Chris Mould

Chris Mould went to art school at the age of sixteen. During this time, he did various jobs, from delivering papers to washing-up and cooking in a kitchen. He has won the Nottingham Children's Book Award and the Swiss Prix Enfantaisie.

He loves his work and likes to write and draw the kind of books that he would have liked to have on his shelf as a boy. He is married with two children and lives in Yorkshire.

THIS BOOK IS THE PROPERTY OF

. . . .

PIRATES 'N' PISTOLS
By Chris Mould

First published in hardback in 2012 by Hodder Children's Books,
First published in paperback in 2013
338 Euston Road, London, NW1 3BH

Hodder Children's Books Australia,
Level 17/207 Kent Street, Sydney, NSW 2000

A catalogue record of this book is available from the British Library.

ISBN: 978 0 340 99935 6

Printed in Italy

Hodder Children's Books is a division of Hachette Children's Books
An Hachette UK Company
www.hachette.co.uk

Pirates 'n' Pistols

CHRIS MOULD

Ten
Swashbuckling
Pirate Tales

Ahoy there, landlubber!

What brings you aboard? Beggin' your pardon, but these murky waters ain't for the faint-hearted and if I were you I'd turn around and keep my boots on dry land.

Not convinced, eh? Well, sit yerself down on that there apple barrel and pin back those ears. When we reach the open sea I'll tell you all the pirate tales I know: walking the plank and digging for gold; seafaring crooks and clashing blades.

And if that don't frighten yer back ashore, you're welcome anytime! Hang onto yer hat my friend and watch ye don't go overboard...

Contents

Davy Jones'Locker

By Chris Mould

ere's a thought. What chills the cold hearts of hardy cut-throats and buccaneers? Surely there is something! When night pulls its cloak across the ocean, what do men at sea talk about? What fills their heads with fear as they sail through the long dark hours?

Let me tell you. When the world was younger and the ports of England brimmed with mariners and traders, a small crooked tavern crouched in the harbour at Bristol dock. The Blind Eye was awash with villains. Every nook and cranny, every table, every spot that held a glass or tankard, was home to some double-deal of one kind or another.

Money changed hands over tabletops, and stolen goods beneath. Handfuls of doubloons were swapped for whispered secrets. Hardened, weatherworn faces shone in the candlelight, as blackguards and scoundrels roared with laughter, and now and then with rage, as they crossed swords and some man's blood ran red across the stone floor.

For the most part, it felt as if the whole of the pirate world was held in the arms of that little old tavern. You could go so far as to say that if you weren't a drinker at The Blind Eye, you were no one!

And what about the landlord? Crooked as the worst of them, and always happy in bad company, as long as the beer flowed freely and money was laid on the counter. Short in the legs he was, but broad in the back, with arms like tree trunks and a head like a slab of meat. It was said he was scared of no man and he thought nothing of using blade or bullet to settle an argument.

So let me take you to The Blind Eye late one summer's evening, when the sun had baked the harbour dry and all the seamen were drinking heavily to quench their thirst. As daylight faded, candlelight spilled out from the tavern windows onto the cobbled street and the noise of quarrelling kept the world awake. There was a fine commotion that night.

A well-known crew had returned from sea. They came with riches, yes. But whose? That was always the first question. Under the flickering light, the treasures were passed around. Everyone was interested and several gasped at what they saw. Many of the treasures were marked with the name: DAVY JONES.

Any sailor worth his sea salt knew about Davy Jones. He was a well-respected sailor and a navigator among seafaring men. A character who was neither friend nor foe to the pirate world, but much admired by all. So to hear that he'd been attacked and robbed made everyone feel uncomfortable. There was sneaking respect for a man who could always find his way home from the darkest corners of the world.

'Davy Jones was the best seaman the seven seas has ever known,' someone whispered.

But business is business. There was no room for finer feelings among the heaving crowd of villains at The Blind Eye. Davy Jones lay dead upon the seabed, shifting endlessly in the ocean currents and everything he ever owned was bought and sold. Such is the way of the pirate world.

A few months later, when that hot summer was as vague a memory as Davy Jones himself, the same pirate crew went missing. They had set sail against the advice of their mates at The Blind Eye. Shortly after their departure, the autumn winds blew wild and strong and there were violent storms. Winter came and there was still no sign of the missing men.

When days are short there is not much fun to be had for the sea crook. If he has been lucky enough to return home, he will escape to the inns and make plans for when good weather returns and he can set sail again. Scheming and plotting is the order of the day and great care is taken to find out where the rich local traders have planned to travel in the coming spring. Sometimes a young lad might be hired to eavesdrop among the merchants, or to steal private letters sending details of their movements.

So, allow me to take you to The Blind Eye once more. Except this time, it was in the full grip of winter. A flurry of snow had dusted the cobbles outside and a fire roared all day long in the tavern. The Blind Eye was home to much mischief, yet it looked friendly and inviting. I can almost see myself heading inside and sitting by the fire, perhaps with a dish of something warm to line my stomach.

But someone else came to the door that night. He dragged an old sea chest behind him and stopped breathlessly at the doorway to kick the snow from his boots and shake his coat tails dry. Hardened faces turned to catch a glimpse of the visitor. For a short moment he went unrecognised. But looking again at his bedraggled sea-stained state it was soon clear that the man who stood hunched and shivering before them was one of the missing crew.

He was pulled inside and made to sit by the fire upon his old sea chest to warm his bones and spill his tale. A drink was placed in his hand but he had neither the will nor the strength to raise it to his lips. Food was brought, too, great hunks of bread and ham. But no, the man was too dazed to speak or eat, so he was left to dry his boots by the burning logs.

It must have been midnight before he opened his mouth. And when he did, he stared straight ahead, as if somehow he was dreaming the story he told.

'We were sent reeling in a storm and lost all sense of where we headed,' he began. 'The sky was black and great waves threw our ship around like a rag doll. We were pinned to the ratlines, shaking like leaves and drenched in the salt water. The wind held us fast and sliced us through like cold steel. Rain drummed hard across our backs. I have never known a night at sea to be so cruel. Seawater poured across the deck, and with it, came all kinds of rubbish from the ocean depths. Sliding and crashing onto the railings, we clawed our way to the cabin door, battening down the hatches as we went. We served no use on deck and could only save ourselves from more punishment, praying that no harm would come to the masts.

The cabin door swung open violently, and for a breath I thought that the wind might catch it and hurl it into the sea. But together we were able to climb inside and pull the cabin door closed, so that deck water did not pour in after us.

Below, it was dry and a smudge of candlelight lit the room, but outside, the wind shrieked and tore at the wooden bones of our ship.

The storm died out just before dawn. We lay exhausted in our swaying hammocks, and eventually, drifted into uneasy slumber, with only the creak and groan of ropes and timbers to soothe us.

But then something woke us from our sea dreaming. We hastened on deck, fearing the worst. The storm had covered the boards with all kinds of sea wash and water life; shells and stones and timbers. Chains too. Long-rusted, barnacled irons, dragged from the depths. They hung across the deck and up into the ratlines like heavy cobwebs. I ask you, what kind of storm brings up such things from the seabed?

And then we saw him, perched in the rigging like a vulture.

It was old Davy Jones himself, still wearing those same chains we wrapped him in. Dead for sure and white as a sheet, but he was grinning even so. He sat somehow calm and still, despite the freezing temperature, his bony, blue hands clasped at the ropes, and his coat tails dripping.

Terror gripped me by the throat, and for a moment it felt as if the whole world had simply stopped turning.

I can still see him now, grinning and laughing and staring, with the loops of his chains hanging low, and his voice coming to us in a sinister whisper through the sea wind. I can't bear to repeat what he said, for it chills me more to think of his words and I'm frozen to the bone as it is.

The next thing I knew, I was bobbing along in the murky water, clutching onto this old sea chest like a drowned rat. All the men were gone and the ship had upturned and dragged them down to the seabed.

I was spared: but only to warn the pirate world that old Davy Jones wants 'is treasures back. So take good care at sea, gentlemen. Keep your eyes open for the storm that brings old Davy Jones from his locker to take back what you've stole.'

And at that, his eyes snapped shut and he fell face forward into the hearth, stone dead.

And therefore it was left to the company of rogues at The Blind Eye to spread the word. The legend of Davy Jones' locker wound its way around the tavern firesides and ships' cabins of the pirate world. No scoundrel or blackguard, pirate or thief could ever sleep easy again while he remembered that Davy Jones was waiting to get even with him.

So, when I ask you what strikes terror into the cold hearts of cut-throats and buccaneers, you now know his name.

TREASURE ISLAND

(excerpt)

By Robert Louis Stevenson
Adapted by Chris Mould

The Hispaniola was bound for Treasure Island. In the glimmer of the ship's lanterns the crew were manning the capstan bars and taking instructions from Captain Smollett. Squire Trelawney and Doctor Livesey were in their cabin looking over the treasure map, while young Jim Hawkins was on deck. It was his first voyage as cabin boy.

The anchor was drawn up and hung dripping at the bows. The sails began to fill and very soon, dry land flitted by on either side.

Jim Hawkins' sea adventure was about to begin.

The Voyage

There was one man I could not help noticing. His left leg was missing and he used a crutch. I heard the crew call him Barbecue and I soon found out that he was the ship's cook and also went by the name of Long John Silver.

On board ship he carried his crutch round his neck, so that he might have both hands free as he stood. It was quite something to see him wedge the foot of the crutch against a bulkhead and, yielding to every movement of the ship, go about his cooking like someone safe ashore.

He would move about at quite a pace, as quickly as any man. Yet those who had sailed with him before expressed pity to see him reduced to such a state.

'He's no common man, Barbecue,' explained Israel, the coxswain, to me. 'He had good schooling in his young days and can speak like a book when so inclined. And brave as a lion, he is. I seen him grapple four men and knock their heads together.'

All the crew admired and even obeyed him. He had a way of talking to each one that commanded their respect. To me, he was endlessly kind and welcoming and he kept the galley as clean as a new pin; the dishes hanging up burnished bright and his parrot in a cage in one corner. There was something about Long John Silver that told me he was the best of men.

'You're young, you are, Jim Hawkins,' he would say to me, 'but you're as smart as paint. I see that when I first set my eyes on you, and I'll talk to you like a man.'

He introduced me to his parrot. 'Cap'n Flint, I calls him. After the famous pirate.' And the parrot would say over and over, 'Pieces of eight, pieces of eight!' till you wondered that it was not out of breath, or until John threw his handkerchief over the cage.

I shall not relate every detail of the voyage. For the most part it was prosperous and the crew were capable seamen. We had some heavy weather, which only proved the qualities of the Hispaniola and every man on board seemed well content. Double grog was served at the least excuse and there was always a barrel of apples on deck, for anyone who might fancy one.

And insignificant as it might seem, great good was to come of the apple barrel as you shall hear. If it had not been for that, we should have had no word of warning of the treachery that faced us.

This was how it came about.

It was the last day of our outward voyage. We had guessed that at some time that night, or before noon the next day, we would catch sight of Treasure Island. We were heading southwest and had a steady breeze at our side and a quiet sea. The Hispaniola plunged forward, dipping her bowsprit now and then into the waves with a whiff of spray and everyone was in the best of spirits.

Just after sundown, when all my work was over, it occurred to me that I should like an apple. I ran on deck. The watch stood silently on lookout for

Treasure Island and the only sound was the swish of the sea against the bows and the whistle of the man who stood at the helm.

There was scarcely an apple left. So scarce, in fact, that I had got myself bodily into the apple barrel before I found one. But sitting down there in the dark, with the rocking of the ship and the gentle sound of the surf, I fell asleep.

All of a sudden, my slumber was broken when a heavy man sat down nearby with a great thump. The barrel shook as the man leaned against it and I was about to jump up when I heard him speak. It was Silver's voice and before I had heard a dozen words I would no more have revealed myself than I would have jumped over the side of the ship.

I understood then that the lives of all the honest men aboard depended on me alone, and I lay there trembling and listening in the extremes of fear and horror.

What I heard in the apple barrel.

'Flint was Captain,' said Silver. 'I was quartermaster. Aye, I saw that old ship o' Flint's running red with blood and fit to sink with gold.'

'Ah,' cried another voice, that of the youngest hand on board, seemingly full of admiration, 'he was the best of buccaneers, was Flint.'

'I sailed with Edward England first, then Flint. That's my story,' said Silver, 'I dunno where England's men are now but as for Flint's, well, there's most of 'em aboard this ship.

But look here,' he went on, addressing the junior hand. 'You're young, you are, but you're as smart as paint. I see that when I first set my eyes on you, and I'll talk to you like a man.'

You may imagine how I felt when I heard Silver talking in this way! The cunning old rogue spoke to the young hand exactly as he had spoken to me! I think if I had been able, I would have killed him through the barrel, right there and then. Meanwhile, he carried on, little supposing he was overheard.

'Flint's lot was the roughest crew afloat; the devil himself would have feared to go to sea with them,' continued Silver. 'But here's the thing about gentlemen of fortune. They live a rough life and they risk swinging at the gallows, but when a cruise is done there's plenty o' money in their pockets.'

'Well, I'll tell you now,' said the youngster, 'I didn't like the idea half as much until I had this talk with you, John; but you have my hand on it now.'

'Then you're smart and brave,' cried Silver, 'and I never clapped eyes on a finer lad for a gentleman of fortune.' And they clasped hands so heartily that the barrel shook. By now I understood the old traitor. By 'gentleman of fortune' he plainly meant nothing more nor less than a common pirate. And it seemed that the little scene I had overheard was the corruption of one of the last of our honest crew. Is this what Silver had aimed to do with me? To turn me against Captain Smollett, Doctor Livesey and the Squire?

Silver gave a whistle and a third man strolled up and sat among the party. I recognised his voice as that of Israel Hands, our coxswain.

'Listen,' said Israel, immediately. 'Here's what I want to know, Barbecue. How long are we going to wait? I've had my fill o' Captain Smollett, he's maddened me long enough, by thunder.'

'Not until I give the word,' said Silver.

'But when will that be?'

'I'll tell you when! The last moment we can manage, that's when,' cried Silver with some anger. 'Captain Smollett is sailing the blessed ship for us. And who's got the map? The squire and doctor! I don't know where the gold is, do I? No more do you. First, we'll let the squire and doctor find this treasure and help us get it aboard. Then we'll see. If I had my way, I'd let Captain Smollett navigate us half way back home before I'd strike.'

'And what are we to do with 'em?' asked the young hand.

'What do you think?' replied Silver, more calmly. 'Put 'em ashore like maroons? Or cut 'em down like pork? Cos dead men don't bite. Mark you here: I'm an easy man – I'm quite the gentleman, says you; but this time it's serious. Duty is duty, mates. I give my vote – and my vote is death. Wait, is all I say; but when the time comes, let her rip. Only one thing I claim – I claim Squire Trelawney. I'll wring his fool head off his body with these hands.'

And then he added to the young hand, 'Now, you just jump up like a sweet lad and get me an apple.'

You may fancy the terror I was in! If I'd had the strength, I would have leaped out and run for it. But my limbs and heart gave way and I was unable to move.

But Israel stopped him. 'Oh, forget that, John. Let's have a shot of your rum.' And they sent the boy off to for a good measure from Silver's keg.

When the lad returned, one after the other took the pannikin and drank, saying, 'To luck'; and, 'Here's to old Flint'; and Silver himself added in a kind of sing-song voice, 'Here's to ourselves, and hold your luff, plenty of prizes and plenty of duff.'

Just then a brightness fell upon me in the barrel and looking up I found the moon had risen. It was silvering the mizzen top and shining white on the foresail. Almost at the same time, the voice of the look out shouted, 'Land ho!'

It was Treasure Island.

The Tenth Man

By Chris Mould

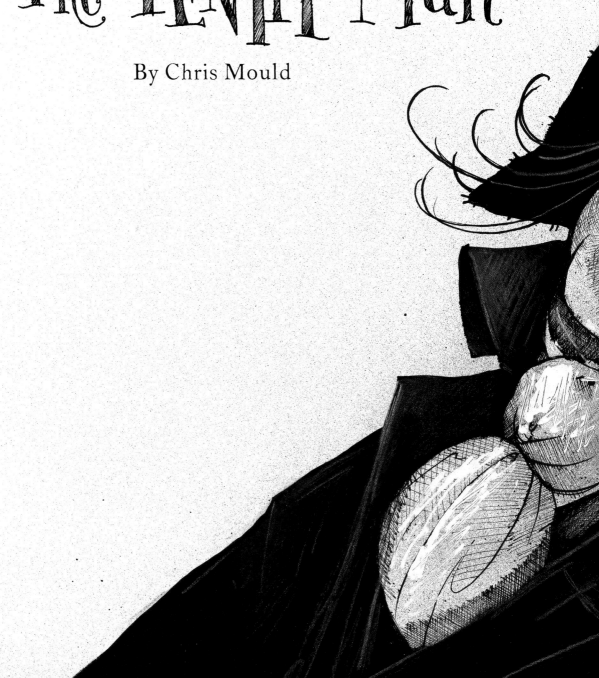

Ten men went to sea. Nine of them knew that one would not return.

The first of the ten was Sneerstout. Another eight of them were a crew of cut-throats he had gathered at the docks. They were young wastrels, looking for work at sea and not worrying about the company they kept as long as their journey brought them handfuls of gold, and there was free grog and wild adventure ahead.

Sneerstout was the worst of pirates, the mad type with nothing to lose. A crazy maverick who would stop at nothing, reckless and thoughtless with every breath and without a speck of compassion or common decency.

He eyed his crew over and matched his hulking frame alongside each of them, one by one, making sure he had the upper hand of each man. He didn't want mutiny when the crew saw his riches. If things turned sour, he wanted to be sure he could deal with the boldest of them. But no one came near to his huge frame.

'Now, here's the deal,' he began, telling them curtly what the job would be. He wanted a crew to take him on a trip and bring him back again. There was work to be done when they got there. Hard work. Digging. And he agreed a price for the whole voyage, there and then. But there was to be no cut of the riches. They all belonged to Sneerstout. And he warned that the last man who laid claim to a share of Sneerstout's gold was still lying on the seabed.

And so to the tenth man. To be blunt, the tenth man wasn't needed. The Octopus was a fine ship; but a small one, with just enough room for the crew that Sneerstout had hired. So why was this extra man aboard?

It was the night before the Octopus set sail. The crew were getting the ship ready to leave, having already brought their own belongings aboard, when a gentleman appeared on the quay. He was smartly dressed in a frock coat and lace and he carried his bags with him. He seemed out of place among the dockworkers and fishermen.

'Permission to come aboard, Sir,' he hollered and set off up the gangplank without waiting for a reply.

Sneerstout stood before him with his hands held at the hip, but Doctor Percival seemed not the slightest bit overawed by the might of the man. He peered over his glasses and smiled.

'Ah, there you are, my fine fellow,' he said. 'Allow me to introduce myself. My name is Doctor Percival and I am a scientist and botanist. A student of plants.' And he went on to explain that he wanted to go in search of new species to create medicines for his practice. Not being a seafaring man, he knew nothing of the oceans and sailing and so he was looking for a ship's company to take him abroad.

Sneerstout snorted and jeered at the man. He was not a transport service and he cared little for Doctor Percival's quest. And because Sneerstout didn't feel like taking the doctor, he was asked to leave the ship. But money talks, and Sneerstout was a man to listen to it.

The doctor made him a handsome offer to come on board. And it was even more handsome by the time Sneerstout had doubled and trebled it.

And so, odd as it seemed to the rest of the crew, Doctor Percival joined the men on board.

The journey began well. The weather was bright and a good wind sent the vessel on its way. The men were in good spirits and even Sneerstout seemed to relax as they sailed smoothly under a hot sun across the endless ocean.

It has to be logged that Doctor Percival spent most of his time below deck. He stood at the helm when they left port but only for a short time. It was soon obvious that he was a hopeless sailor and he was very seasick. He explained to Sneerstout that he would be spending time below deck to recover, and to everyone's amusement, from then on he only ventured out when the sea was at its calmest, looking pale and drawn.

Doctor Percival kept his distance from the crew. He ate alone in his cabin and spent much of his time writing in his diary along the way. Now and then, he would surface to take in a gulp of sea air and bid the crew a good day. But before long the rocking and swaying of the boat would send him scurrying below again.

The other nine men spent their days at the capstan bars and the helm, the rigging and the crow's nest. At night they retired to the cabin and made foolery, or sat drinking Sneerstout's grog and listening to tales of his wild adventures.

Sneerstout boasted how he had gained his riches and many of his stories of the seven seas made uneasy listening, even to his crew, for his tales were grim and tasteless, full of mindless cruelty and sudden death.

In the days ahead, the journey drew to a close and land appeared out of the ocean. Excitement filled the deck. It had been an agreeable journey and the prospect of riches filled Sneerstout with excitement.

I shall not bore you with details of how the ship's company came ashore and made camp, but in short, there was soon a fire burning and wood smoke curling up from the beach. Shelter was assembled while the boat listed lazily in the bay, its anchor pitted in the white sand.

Then Doctor Percival made an announcement. He was delighted to feel his feet touching dry land (although he was already dreading the journey home) and if they would excuse him, he would set about hunting for plants. Immediately he took out glass bottles and tubes, began setting up his instruments and he soon set out on his quest.

Doctor Percival came late to the camp. He was quiet and made nods here and there, politely thanking the crew for the food and drink.

The following day was the one that brought surprise. The crew awoke to see Sneerstout pacing up and down, measuring his steps and looking at his map. He spent a good while mumbling and grumbling to himself and reading through his papers over breakfast.

By midday, his crew were sweating as they dug a huge hole, as deep as a man is high. But it was not deep enough. Sneerstout was cursing. 'Keep going, you scum,' he yelled. 'And careful. There's gold in that pit.'

At long last, the shovel speared a chunk of half-rotted wood.

A ship's casket showed itself, emerging slowly from the sandy earth. It took all nine of them and all their strength to haul the container out of the hole with ropes and pulleys, such was the weight of the prize.

It was at that moment that Doctor Percival appeared. He was reading his notes and he seemed not to notice the huge, now empty hole, until someone shouted, 'Ahoy there, landlubber! Watch where you're putting your feet!' He turned to greet them.

'Well, well, gentlemen! My goodness. It seems you have had a better day than me,' he said, peering over the top of his spectacles.

Now, as I said at the beginning, Sneerstout was the worst of pirates. He was reckless, unpredictable and cruel. But this story is not only about him. It is also a tale of those who take us by surprise. Whom we would never suspect of ill doing. The ones who perhaps we had seen as mild and gentle. Trustworthy, even.

Doctor Percival took a shovel and dug it firmly into the back of Sneerstout, sending him head first into the empty pit. And then, amid his muffled shouts and screams, the doctor filled in the hole with the help of the crew from the Octopus. He also threw in his useless plants and notebooks and scientific instruments, as they carried on shovelling and kicking the dirt into the grave.

Then Doctor Percival turned to his men and shook their hands. A job well done deserves a fine reward and there was enough gold in the casket to share between everyone, and enough grog aboard the Octopus to last the journey home.

The GOLD BUG

(excerpt)

By Edgar Allan Poe

After claiming to have been bitten by a scarab beetle made from pure gold, William Legrand has become obsessed with the hunt for Captain Kidd's treasure. Accompanied by his assistant and a companion, who are convinced he is merely going insane, they embark on an expedition. As we join them, Legrand is convinced he has worked out the very spot where the treasure lies.

Again we set to work with our spades. I was exhausted but I had become too excited to stop what I was doing. I dug eagerly, and now and then, caught myself actually looking with something that resembled expectation, for the fancied treasure. The vision of it had almost sent my companion Mister Legrand crazy.

When we had been at work perhaps an hour and a half, we were again interrupted by the violent howling of our dog. Our assistant, Jupiter, made an attempt to muzzle him but he resisted furiously, leaping into the hole and tearing up the earth frantically with his claws.

Within moments he had uncovered a mass of human bones, forming

two complete skeletons, intermingled with several buttons of metal, and what appeared to be the dust of decayed garments. One or two further strokes of a spade upturned the blade of a large Spanish knife, and as we dug further, three or four loose pieces of gold and silver came to light.

At the sight of these, the joy of Jupiter could scarcely be restrained, but Mister Legrand wore an air of extreme fear and disappointment. He urged us, however, to keep going, and the words were hardly uttered when I stumbled and fell forward, having caught the toe of my boot in a large ring of iron that lay half buried in the loose earth.

We now worked in earnest, and never did I pass ten minutes of more intense excitement. During this time we unearthed a chest of wood, perfectly preserved. It must have been just over a metre long and was secured by bands of wrought iron, riveted and forming a kind of trelliswork over the whole of it. On each side of the chest, near the top, were three rings of iron – six in all – and clearly, by means of these,

six persons could take a firm hold and lift it.
Our greatest efforts could only move it
slightly in its bed and we immediately saw the
impossibility of lifting so great a weight.
Luckily, the only fastenings to the lid were
two sliding bolts. These we drew back –
trembling and panting with anxiety.
In an instant, a treasure of immense value lay
gleaming before us. As the rays of our lanterns
fell into the chest, there flashed
upwards, from a confused heap
of gold and jewels, a glow
and a glare that absolutely
dazzled our eyes.

I shall not attempt to describe the feelings with which I gazed. Amazement was, of course, the strongest. Legrand appeared exhausted with excitement and could utter only a few words. Jupiter was thunderstruck. He fell upon his knees in the pit, and, burying his naked arms up to the elbows in gold, let them remain there, as if enjoying the luxury of a bath.

It was now necessary for us to think how to take the treasure from its hole and much time was spent in trying to work out this difficult problem. Finally, we lightened the chest by taking out two thirds of its gold and jewels. Only then were we able to pull it from the earth.

Everything we'd taken out was hidden amongst the brambles and the dog left to guard it. Jupiter gave strict orders that the dog should not move from the spot, or open its mouth, until our return. We then made for home as fast as we could with the chest, and after an exhausting struggle reached our hut in safety at one o'clock in the morning. After some rest and supper we set out for the hills again with three stout sacks and retrieved the remainder of the booty, reaching the hut again just as the first streaks of the dawn gleamed over the treetops in the east.

We were now worn out with effort; but intense excitement kept us from sleeping and after dozing uneasily for three or four hours, we woke and began to examine our treasure.

The chest had been full to the brim and we spent the whole day and the greater part of the next night looking carefully at its contents. Everything had been shovelled in without order, and sorting it all, piece by piece, we found ourselves possessed of even greater wealth than we had at first supposed.

In coin there was more than four thousand dollars: French, German and Spanish money, with a few English guineas. There were several large and heavy coins, so worn that we could make nothing of their inscriptions. There were diamonds, some of them exceedingly large and fine – a hundred and ten in all. Rubies, emeralds and opals, all broken from their settings and thrown loose in the chest. The settings were there too, but they had been beaten with hammers, as if to prevent identification. Besides all this, there were a vast quantity of solid gold ornaments, earrings, chains and crucifixes.

We guessed the entire contents of the chest that night was worth a million and a half dollars.

'There is only one thing which puzzles me,' I said, turning to Mister Legrand. 'Why were those skeletons in the hole?'

'That is a question I am no more able to answer than you.' Legrand looked troubled as he spoke. 'There seems, however, only one possible reason – and yet it is so dreadful that it is hard to believe anyone capable of such cruelty and violence.

Captain Kidd – if indeed he did squirrel away this treasure – would have had some help in doing so. But he may have thought it necessary to get rid of anyone who shared his secret. Perhaps a couple of blows with a mattock would have been enough while his helpers were busy in the pit; or maybe it took a dozen – who can tell?'

Our mood of happiness and excitement drained away at his words, and the glittering gold and jewels, riches beyond our wildest dreams, seemed suddenly menacing and evil. Who could tell how many lives they had already claimed? How many more were doomed to die before our journey was over?

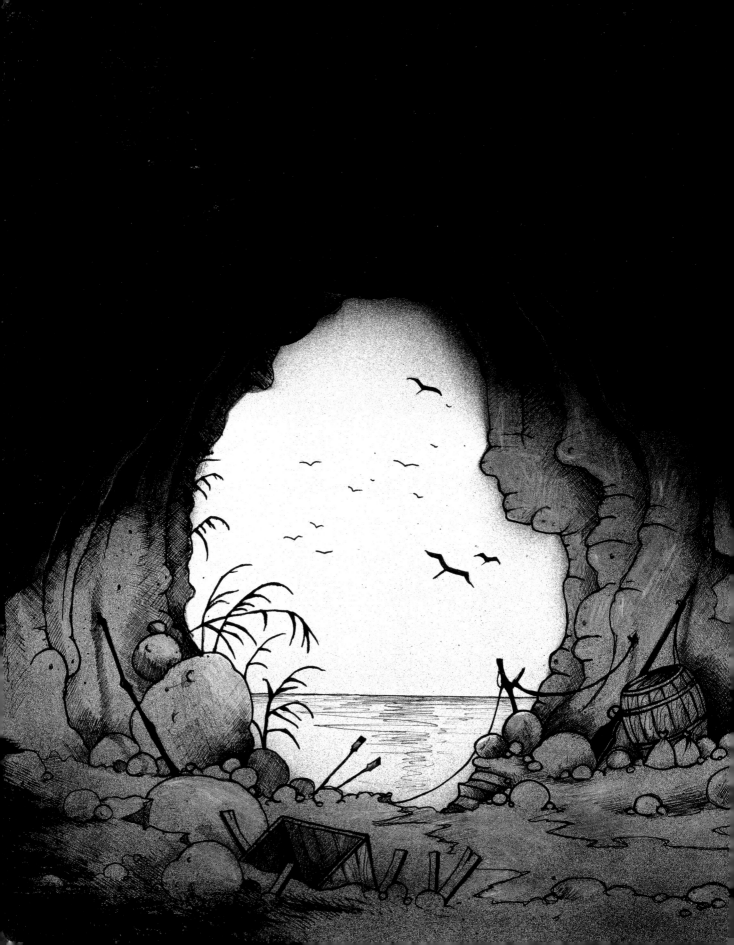

DEAD MAN'S INK

By Chris Mould

You would have known Tyrrell Dukes anywhere. Tattoos scribbled their way from his temples to his toes. Covered in them he was, and even in later years he looked fearsome. He wasn't big, not by any means, but he was hard and sharp, with a meanness in his glare, and a strange way of walking which was probably the result of an old injury. No doubt he had musket shot lodged somewhere about him.

His reputation went before him and Dukes was known as unpredictable and dangerous.

A rumour went about that when his tattooist had finished the last design on his body, Dukes shot him dead, right there and then – and he had a poor wife and children, too.

But the strangest thing about Dukes was that he kept a huge bear on board his ship. Whilst in port, both he and the bear drank alongside one another at the dockside taverns, standing together at the bar. The bear would be on its hind legs in a chain harness, so that it could be controlled with a tug, if need be.

For sure it was quite a sight, and even the boldest of seafaring rogues was afraid to pick a quarrel with the man. They would clear most places as soon as they entered, he with his tattoos, and the bear on its hind legs.

But to get to the point. It was well known that old Dukes possessed a map to a local island, where he had buried his untold riches. It was said that a pit wasn't good enough for all his treasures. No, it was reckoned he had dug a labyrinth of tunnels, a maze of darkened passages designed to

trap anyone stupid enough to venture inside. Maybe those tunnels even snaked beyond the island, under the sea. Rumours persisted about his crew, too. It was said that once they had dug the tunnels, the bear had killed them, one by one, so that Dukes' secret remained safe.

But one night, after too much drink, Dukes got into a foul temper and beat the bear with its own chains. The two fought and at the end of it, the man lay horribly wounded. And as he had always promised, he took his secret to the grave without uttering another word. The bear lumbered out of the inn on four legs, dragging its chains behind it and was never seen again.

Despite his wounds, they smartened up Dukes for his funeral. He wore a lace-trimmed shirt and necktie with buckled boots and a blue swallowtail coat. His hands were crossed over his chest; but even though the undertaker tried his best, Dukes had a horrible expression upon his face that couldn't be altered.

Nothing could have been more suitable that morning than the thunderous cloud that hung over the sea and drifted inland to the hillside graves standing like crooked teeth on the grassy knoll. A huddle of rogues stood at the graveside. The mud clogged their feet and the rain continued relentlessly soaking them to the bone as they waited for Dukes' coffin to be lowered into the hole.

If the truth be known, the only reason those pirates were there was so that they would know where to return with their spades and shovels. And the soil was still fresh in its hole, when it was turned out again the next moonlit night. The pockets of Dukes' swallowtail coat were fingered, as were the insides of his hat and the cuffs of his frilled shirt. Someone inspected his boots and realising they were a good pair, replaced them with his own. Dukes' body was propped awkwardly by his own headstone, while the coffin itself was carefully examined. Nothing! The small casket at his feet was smashed open; but except for a worthless necklace, a handful of silver and a portrait of his mother, there was not a single item in Dukes' possession that looked like a map.

By now, Dukes' map was notorious and the local villains were desperate to find it. The hovel he had called his home was turned inside out and searched from top to bottom, from cobwebby attic to damp basement. Nothing.

The map had to be somewhere.

A few years went by, and the story became a fireside favourite at the inns. It was told and re-told how an old tattooed pirate called Dukes had a treasure map and fought with his own bear. It must have been told a thousand times before it was at last heard by someone who knew the answer to the riddle!

One evening, the tattooist's widow took a job at a nearby inn. Time had passed since her husband's death and her children were grown up, but she could not forget the man who had killed her husband. Though she could not name him for sure, she knew that her husband's final customer had been tattooed head to toe and that he had made this odd request.

He had wanted a map drawn across his chest!

Once they heard this, those pirates stormed out of the inn right there and then, and set off to the grassy knoll where the tombstones stood. And not for the first time, the soil in Dukes' grave was turned out by those rogues, who burrowed like mad dogs until they hit his crumbling, wooden coffin.

But when they opened the lid under the flickering candlelight, they realised at once that all hope was lost. For old Dukes was nothing but dust and bones. Where once his secret had been upon his chest, nothing now remained but the tattered remains of his blue coat with his pale ribs showing through.

And the gold?

Some say that the bear was the only one that knew. They liked the idea that now he lives in well fed comfort somewhere under the sun with servants fussing around him. Many treasure-seekers claimed to have dug up Dukes' treasure, but if as many men had found it as claim, there would have been gold to fill a fleet of ships.

And what do I think? Well, I like to think it still sits there, sleeping silently in the darkness of those unseen tunnels, waiting patiently to be discovered like an unopened present.

And maybe one day, some lucky soul like you will chance upon it?

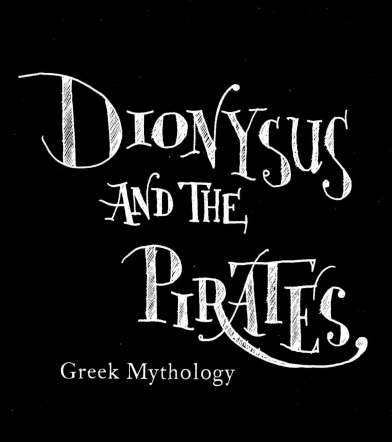

Dionysus and the Pirates

Greek Mythology

Some tales are harder to swallow than others. With good reason, too. Perhaps the storyteller is not to be trusted (not meaning me, of course!), or maybe the listener already knows better. Sometimes, the facts just seem like plain madness. Well, I can promise you that though this is a wild tale, every word of it is true.

Dionysus was a Greek god and like most of the Greek gods, he could change shape at will. When he was in his mortal shape, he looked, at first glance, like any other young man. He was handsome and strong, with long dark hair, but his eyes were bright as stars and his smile would turn your blood to ice. As this tale begins, he was wandering alone on the island of Naxos.

I've lived to regret my last journey at sea and I suppose, deep down, I always knew I would. A few months ago, I was penniless and homeless and I'd taken the only choice I had and joined a band of pirates. I was starving and in no position to be choosy. Aboard ship, at least I had a place to lay my head and food in my stomach.

I hoped for a swift journey, good fortune and though I knew not what lay ahead, I believed that my future would be brighter than it had been.

When we first set sail, the sky was clear and the sea calm and our crew rowed eagerly with a blistering sun on their backs. I had come aboard as helmsman and so as we moved out to sea, I stood at the rear and steered us forwards. There was an excitement that comes with the start of a new journey and though I did not know the crew, they seemed like loyal, good shipmates.

We were heading across the bay towards Naxos, when we spied a young man from our boat as it dipped and bobbed on the surf. He was walking alone on the headland. 'He looks like the son of a rich king,' I heard someone say.

Then the captain cried, ' A chance, lads! It's an open door to untold riches!' Foolishly, without knowing anything about this mysterious and beautiful young man, we headed to shore and seized him. Then my mates dragged him aboard our boat.

I tried to stop them. I told them that he was no ordinary king's son. What did they know about him? But they laughed and pushed me to the ground. What fools they were!

Our captain taunted me. 'Coward!' he cried. 'This is a rich man's son who will bring us a rich ransom.'

But when they brought the young man on board, I saw at once that I was right. Something in his calm, commanding look, his walk, his voice told me that this was no ordinary mortal. I begged the crew to set him free, wildly grabbing their arms. But they punched me and kicked me. One seized me by the throat and would have stabbed me to death if the captain had not pushed him away. I know now, I was lucky to live.

Excited with their success, my shipmates tried to tie up their captive. 'Let's see how he gets out of this!' they jeered, wrenching his arms together and loading them with chains. But every time they locked the irons, they dropped uselessly to the ground. Dionysus did not move. He sat there smiling and watching as the chains fell in a heap at his feet.

I shook with terror. 'This is no mortal man!' I cried. 'We have captured one of the gods! Set him free or we are cursed.'

But the captain was stubborn. 'Only dogs are scared. Brave men have nothing to fear,' he cried. 'Set sail – and if any coward disobeys, I'll throw him overboard myself!' The men lifted the sails and as they caught the wind, the ship slid out into deep waters.

Dionysus stared at him silently and the ghost of a smile played on his lips.

It is often said that deep waters bring deep trouble and as the land became a hazy blot under the midday sun, strange things began to happen aboard the vessel.

At the top of the mast, a green shoot sprang out and grew rapidly down the sail. Before the terrified eyes of the crew, tendrils of a grapevine multiplied and spread across the deck.

Leaves, blossoming flowers and then fruit burst out from every corner of the ship and the air was heavy with their scent.

Dionysus sat terrifyingly still, his eyes shining like lights. Slowly, a trickle of wine oozed across the deck and soon it poured like rich, red blood, puddling warm around our feet and ankles.

Still the captain refused to give in. 'When this man is ready, he will tell us where his wealth lies. Then there'll be no talk of gods.'

But by now the crew were scared. They turned their backs on their captain and begged me to turn the ship around and head for shore, desperate to set their dangerous captive free.

It was too late. Before the terror-struck men could move or think, the young man's bare feet became huge claws, his teeth turned into ripping fangs and his long, dark hair became a tawny mane. Dionysus had changed into a lion. With one blow of his powerful paw he crushed the captain and tore him to pieces.

The crew could not speak to beg or plead, they were frozen to the spot. But at that moment, the lion bared its teeth and snarled at them.

Suddenly, it was as if the crew were released from a spell and they ran for their lives, slipping and slithering on the decks awash with wine and the captain's blood. One by one, they clambered over the railings and threw themselves into the heaving sea. But as they jumped, their forms changed. They grew fins and tails, their faces were not their own. The god had turned them, each and every one, into dolphins.

My heart was beating in my throat. I knew I had to leave the ship or

be eaten alive, but I was terrified of losing my human shape like the rest of the crew. I closed my eyes and threw myself into the sea.

To my astonishment, the god spared me. As I leapt, I heard his voice whisper, 'I am Dionysus, whom some call the god of wine. My mother is Semele, daughter of Cadmus but my father is Zeus, the king of the gods.'

I knew nothing else until I woke upon a comfortable bed inside a darkened room, a fisherman at my side. He had found me upon the shore, more dead than alive. I knew then that the gods had been with me, but, for sure, I had taken my final journey at sea.

Cross-Legged Jack

By Chris Mould

erhaps you would not think much of Cross-legged Jack if you saw him. After all, he could fit in a teacup. He sits on an old chest and in his hands he holds a broadsword. One clasps the handle firmly and the other touches the shining blade between two fingers. A sack at his feet is opened slightly and you can just see a glimpse of the riches within. It is said he was a corsair. A pirate from the ancient world.

At one time, Cross-legged Jack had sat in an old shop window, amongst the odds and ends that gathered dust and cobwebs. Often, boys would go and stare at him through the glass and dream of taking him home.

It was only a matter of time before Cross-legged Jack found his way onto a bedroom shelf. He sat confidently with his sword held aloft and his hands poised in anticipation of using his blade, guarding a whole army of storybooks and keeping intruders at bay.

But then, without explanation or reason, he was discarded. It appeared he had lost his charm and he was quickly passed on to another and then another... Each liked the look of Cross-legged Jack but to have him in their possession was something else.

The boys remembered long nights of ships at sea and digging for treasure. Trapped in pitch-blackness, straining for the sight of gold, seawater rushing in at their feet. And it was so real that they were sure they could smell the salt water and feel the roughened grains of sand between their toes.

Sometimes, they held a whip over many men. Whilst they were held in chains, they struck them, as they pulled on the oars of a pirate galley. Gold coins bulged out of sacks and spilled across the decks.

Always, those boys would wake with a start out of one of those terrible dreams, shivering and shaking in the darkness and it would take several moments to realise that they were safe in their beds. The next day would be spent feeling listless and tired. Deep in their bones, they knew Cross-legged Jack was cursed.

And ever since, each boy has wondered – where is he now? Whose sleep has he stolen, as he sits, eyes shining in the darkness, burying his wild tales of pirate gold into their unsuspecting dreams?

Mochimitsu's Music

Traditional Japanese Tale

What do you think it would take to defeat a crew of murdering sea bandits? And imagine this, you must do it alone! No army of soldiers by your side. No broadsword or musket. No weapons of any kind. What then?

Well, that's exactly what Mochimitsu faced. So sit back and listen, because this story tells how he survived a pirate attack, entirely by himself.

When Mochimitsu was a boy, the young ones would head off into the Tottori forest looking for bits of fallen timber to make into swords and shields. Then they would play until sundown racing up and down the streets, their wooden weapons clashing against each other.

But from the beginning, Mochimitsu knew he was different. As he watched the other boys playing like little warriors, he knew that fighting was not for him.

What Mochimitsu loved more than anything was music. So while the others fought and argued over their wooden swords, he would slip away and listen under the window of a young violinist. She played so well and he loved the music so much that sometimes he would sit there for hours, listening in the darkness. Then one night, she found him lying there asleep.

'I'm so sorry,' said Mochimitsu, 'I fell asleep to your beautiful music. Please forgive me.'

He thought she would be angry, but she was charmed by his simple admiration, and she offered to let him play. Mochimitsu was a poor boy, and he had never expected to touch a violin, much less play one. But from the first moment he held a violin in his hands, he knew it was what he had always wanted.

A violin is not an easy instrument to play. 'It's a lifetime's work,' the young violinist warned him. But Mochimitsu was not worried. Every day he visited her and she taught him a little more, delighted with the enthusiasm of her young pupil.

He worked hard, earning pocket money so that one day he might buy his own violin. And when he wasn't working, he practised. The other boys laughed at him as they played with their swords and shields.

'We will be great warriors,' they boasted. 'And what will you be?'

But Mochimitsu did not mind. He just smiled and answered that he would be a great musician.

The boys grew up and became soldiers, but Mochimitsu went on practising his violin. He seemed to have an almost magical touch and now people stopped simply to listen to the beauty of his music.

The soldiers, now grown men, still teased him. 'What use is music?' they asked. Music could not win a war or solve a dispute. But Mochimitsu did not mind. He just smiled and said that perhaps it was better to create something than destroy it.

Before long, his music became famous and he was invited all over the world. He sailed far and wide in his own small boat and there was nothing he liked better than to sit on deck, practising his violin, his music drifting

across the ocean while the sea breeze drew his sails onward.

But one morning he awoke to a sea fog and dangerous company. A
large pirate junk was heading toward his boat, but the mist was so thick
that Mochimitsu could not even make out where the sky ended and sea
began. He climbed up the mast, but his flickering torch only served to
smudge the light further.

And then the pirates attacked. First their voices, and then the clang of
steel betrayed their knives and swords. Now Mochimitsu could see them;
their piercing eyes and pointed blades glittering through the mist. Hands
on rope and timber, blades held between the teeth, evil men emerged from
the eerie half-light and clambered onto Mochimitsu's boat.

'What do you want from me?' shouted Mochimitsu from the top of
the mast. 'I am a poor man. I have no riches for you.'

'We want your boat and everything on it,' sneered the pirates, crowding onto the deck, and looking in vain for him. No matter how Mochimitsu pleaded, they promised that once they found him, they would kill him and take everything he had.

He began to panic. He was in great despair. He was no fighting man. A tear welled up in his eye. He had never meant anybody any harm and now he was to die a cruel and pointless death. Perhaps the boys were right, all those years ago in the forest. What good was a violin against cold steel?

By now, there were all manner of noises coming from below him. Barrels and boxes were upturned. Rigging was cut and sails slashed as the pirates searched uselessly for gold.

Mochimitsu looked at his violin and he said to himself, 'I will play my last piece of music. It will be the best I have ever played and then I will die a happy man.'

He closed his eyes and his ears to the sounds of the pirates and began to play. As he did so, all his worries drifted away through the fog. His mind tuned into his music and all else became unimportant.

But then strangest thing happened. The pirates paused. Glorious music was drifting through the fog and they began to listen. It was the most beautiful sound they had ever heard, and so peaceful that it made them feel calm and happy. They put down their weapons and sat quietly around the ship on the barrels and ropes, soaking up the wonderful melodies.

Mochimitsu had not noticed that the mayhem had stopped below him, because he was so engrossed in his music. At last, he played a final note and descended the rigging, ready to go to his death.

He climbed down onto the deck, expecting the pirates to leap on him and cut him to pieces. But they were in a peaceful trance. They shook his hand. Then they thanked him for his music and without saying another word, returned to their boat and departed silently into the mist.

And so I guess that Mochimitsu had the last laugh. Without his music, he would never have single-handedly overcome the pirates and lived to tell the tale.

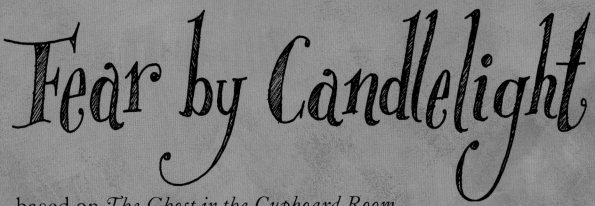

Fear by Candlelight

based on *The Ghost in the Cupboard Room*
by Wilkie Collins

You may laugh as much as you like, but what haunts me the most in all the world is the sight of a bedroom candlestick. I wish it were something more reasonable. A darkened cellar, a coach and horses, or such like. But that is the way it is. It is clear to me now, that the haunting of any man begins with the frightening of him.

Let me tell you how it came to be that the mere sight of a candlestick and candle was enough to reduce me to wide-eyed terror.

I was apprenticed to the sea when I was about as tall as my own walking stick and it was in the year 1819 that I reached the age of twenty-five. During that year there was peace in our part of the world – and not before it was wanted, I can tell you. But there was fighting going on in that old fighting-ground which we seafaring men knew as the Spanish Main.

I was then mate of a brig that belonged to a firm in the city. It drove a general trade in odd, out-of-the-way places, usually far from home. In the year I speak of we carried a cargo of gunpowder for a certain General Bolivar and his men. Nobody knew anything of our instructions when we sailed, except the captain.

I couldn't say how many barrels of powder we had on board, or how much each barrel held – I only know we had no other cargo. The name of the brig was The Good Intent – a strange name you might say for a vessel laden with gunpowder, sent to help a revolution.

The Good Intent was the craziest old tub of a vessel I ever went to sea in. She was laden with two hundred and eighty tons and she had a crew of eight, all told – nothing like as many as we ought have had to work her. Despite this, we were honestly paid our wages and we set that against the chance of foundering at sea and on this occasion, the chance of being blown up into the bargain.

Because of the nature of our cargo, we were harassed with new regulations which we didn't at all like. They related to smoking our pipes and lighting our lanterns. Not a man among us was allowed to have a lighted candle in his hand when he went below.

As is usual in such cases, the captain who made the regulations didn't practise what he preached. When he went to his bed or looked over his charts, he would use a lighted candle, same as he had always done.

The light was a common kitchen candle and it stood in an old battered candlestick. It was the sort with all the lacquer worn off and the tin showing through. For sure it would have been more seaman-like had he used a lamp or lantern, but he stuck to his old candlestick.

We set our course first, for the Virgin Islands in the West Indies; and, after sighting them, we made for the Leeward Islands; and then stood due south, till the lookout saw land. That land was the coast of South America. It had been a wonderful voyage that far. We had lost none of our spars and sails, and not a man among us had been worked to death at the pumps. It wasn't often The Good Intent made such a voyage, I can tell you.

On that evening, it was dark before we closed in on the land. We had wondered why the skipper didn't anchor, but he said, no, he must first show a light at the foretop-masthead, and wait for an answering light on shore. We waited and nothing came. For the best part of an hour nothing happened, and then, instead of seeing a light on shore, we saw a boat coming towards us, rowed by two men.

We hailed them and they answered 'Friends!' and addressed us by our name. They came on board. One handed a note to the skipper informing us that the part of the coast we were on was not safe for discharging our cargo, as spies had been taken and shot in the neighbourhood only the day before. The note was signed by a trustworthy source. It also said that one of the two newcomers was a native pilot, and would safely show us the way to another part of the coast. So we allowed the other man to head back to shore in his boat and let the pilot take charge of our brig.

He took us further out to sea, as his orders were to keep us well out of sight of the shore. We closed in again a little before midnight.

Our pilot was as ill-looking a vagabond as I ever saw, a quarrelsome mongrel who swore at the men in English, till every one of them were ready to pitch him over the side. The skipper kept them quiet as we were forced to make the best of the situation.

Near nightfall, I was unlucky enough to quarrel violently with him.

He wanted to go below with his pipe and I was forced to stop him, of course, because it was contrary to orders. He tried to push past me and I held him back with my hand. I never meant to push him down but somehow, he fell. He picked himself up as quick as lightning, and pulled out a knife. I snatched it out of his hand, slapped his murderous face, and threw his weapon overboard. He gave me one ugly look and walked away.

Eventually, some time between eleven and twelve that night, we dropped anchor. It was pitch dark and there was a dead, airless calm. The skipper was on deck with one of our best men on watch. The rest were below, except the pilot, who coiled himself up on the forecastle.

The skipper whispered to me that he didn't like the look

of things. That is the last thing I remember, before the slow, heavy roll of the brig on the ground swell rocked me off to sleep.

I was awoken by the sounds of a scuffle and a gag was pushed in my mouth. There was a man on my chest and a man on my legs. I was bound hand and foot in half-a-minute. The brig was in the hands of pirates! I heard six heavy splashes in the water, one after another, and I saw the captain stabbed in the heart, followed by a seventh splash.

I was the only one on board not to have been murdered and thrown into sea. Why I was left I couldn't think, till I saw the pilot stoop over me with a lantern, looking to make sure who I was. There was a devilish grin on his face. I knew then that he intended to punish me.

I could neither move nor speak, but I watched the pirates take off the main hatch and go about their work. I heard the sweep of a schooner or other small vessel in the water. It lay alongside us and they began to load our cargo onto her. The pilot came from time to time with his lantern to have another look at me, and to grin and nod in the same devilish way. I do not mind saying that this frightened me a great deal.

Before long, they had shifted a good part of the cargo onto their vessel and they were clearly anxious to be off before daybreak.

While I lay there, I had worked it all out in my mind. It had all been planned. The pilot was a spy and had won our confidence without being

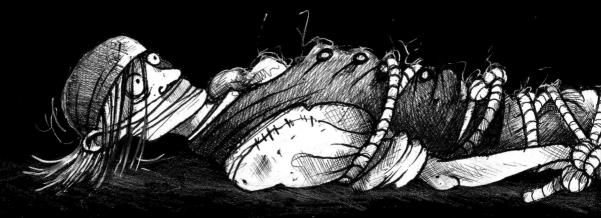

suspected. The pirates must have already known what our cargo was, and arranged to have us anchored for the night in the safest berth for them to surprise us in. And we had paid the penalty of having a small crew and an insufficient watch.

But what of this pilot? What was he going to do with me? It makes my flesh creep to tell you, yet I shall tell you all the same.

The pirates were out of the brig by now, save for our pilot and two others. They helped him to lower me, bound and gagged, into the hold of our ship. I was lashed to it with ropes so that I could turn slightly from one side to the other but not change my place. Then they left me.

I lay in the dark with my heart thumping as if it was going to jump right out of my body. In about five minutes the pilot came down into the hold, alone.

He carried the skipper's candlestick and a sharpened tool in one hand, and a long, thin twist of cotton yarn in the other. The candle was lit and placed about two feet from my face. It was a feeble light but enough to show a dozen barrels of gunpowder positioned around me. At that moment, I began to suspect what he had in mind. Horror took hold of me from head to foot and sweat poured from me like running water.

He bored a hole into the barrel with the sharpened tool and the gunpowder came trickling out, black as hell. He dripped it into the hollow of his hand, and rubbed it into

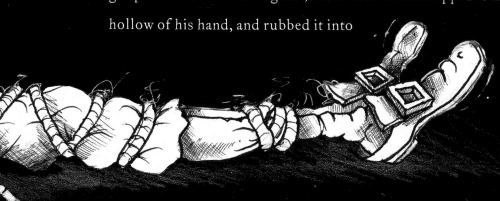

the cotton yarn, which he used to stop up the hole in the barrel. Next, he took the other end of the blackened yarn and ran it alongside of me to the lighted candle, where he tied it carefully, winding the yarn around the candle several times to make a slow fuse.

He checked to see that my ropes were secure. And then he put his face close to mine and whispered, 'I'll watch you blow to pieces with this brig!'

The next thing I knew he was gone and I watched the hatch close above me. A blink of daylight glimmered through. I heard the water lapping around the schooner and then it was carried off as the wind filled its sails.

While those sounds were in my ears, my eyes were fixed on the candle. Left to itself, I guessed it would burn for six or seven hours. But the cotton yarn was twisted around it about a third of the way down and therefore the flame would only take a couple of hours to reach it. And so there I lay, gagged and bound, watching my life burning down with the candle. I was utterly alone, and with every second that passed, the moment drew nearer when I was doomed to be blown to atoms.

As any other man would in my place, I made frantic efforts to free my hands. In the mad panic I was in, I cut my flesh with the ropes as if they had been knife blades; but I made no progress. There was even less chance of freeing my legs. The gag was a terrible enemy to me. I could barely breathe and in my terror, I felt as if I was suffocating.

I gave in and lay quiet, gaining my breath again; my eyes straining at the candle all the time. Perhaps I could blow out the candle

with a blast of air from my nostrils? But no – it was not near enough. I
tried and tried, but in the end I lay quiet again; always with my eyes fixed
on the candle and the candle, seemingly, staring right back at me. The
length of the tallow between the flame and the cotton thread, which was
the length of my life, became shorter and shorter.

Was there a chance that some boat might come by? Through the chink
in the hatch I could see that it was almost daylight. But the coast had
seemed uninhabited. Who would be passing at this hour?

I gave in once more and lay still. Not a sound could I hear except now
and then, the faint cry of a seabird and the creak of the brig's crazy old
spars, as she rolled gently from side to side in the swell.

An hour and a quarter. The candlewick looked as if it might fall off
soon. If it did, and it fell upon the cotton yarn, I would have all of ten
minutes to live. And I began to think what blowing up would feel
like, or indeed, if I would know anything at all when it
happened.

I struggled hard to force my eyes away from the slow, murdering flame. I had many thoughts in those moments, and the flame of the candle burned them all up in an instant.

I caught myself laughing. Yes! Laughing! But for the gag, I would have screamed with laughter. I had just enough sense left to realise that my own horrid mirth was a sign of growing madness.

I made one last effort to drag my eyes from the candle. It was the hardest fight I had had yet. And I lost it. The flame took hold of my eyes as fast as the ropes had hold of my hands. The candle shortened to a couple of inches or less.

How much longer? Half an hour? Fifty minutes? Twenty?

I saw many things in the following minutes. Visions of pure madness, and all the images mixed up together, as if in some crazy dream. My mother sat in her armchair, with slow matches made of cotton yarn burning all around her face, instead of her own grey hair. The pilot with his hands dripping in gunpowder, his face shining red like a hot fiery sun, and the brig, glittering in fire and mist. Everything was red and black and glowing with unearthly light.

I remember nothing else until I woke. There were two men at my side and a doctor, at the foot of my bed. It was about seven in the morning. My sleep (or what seemed like sleep) had lasted more than eight months. I was among my own countrymen in the island of Trinidad. What I said and did in those eight months, I have never known and never shall. All I remember is the doctor watching me with quiet sympathy as I stared around me, dazed, like a man awakened from the sleep of death.

What had happened?

The captain of an American ship had spied the brig, and ordered his mate to launch a boat to look into the matter and report back.

What the mate found was a deserted ship and when he boarded he saw a gleam of candlelight through the chink in the hatchway. The flame was within seconds of touching the slow match. If he had not had the sense to cut the cotton yarn in two before touching the candle, the whole brig would have blown sky high. The very act of putting out the candle would have ignited the slow fuse. So cutting it in two saved both our lives – and probably the American ship as well, for it was too near to have escaped the blast.

So as I say, I was saved at the last moment. I'm all right now as you can see. But I'm a little shaken having the told the story – a little shaken, that's all.

87

The Jewel of Bengal

By Chris Mould

The Strait of Malacca is a narrow strip of water that makes a vital shipping link between India and China. Cargo ships move endlessly backwards and forwards. Rivers and small islands scatter along its length and mangrove swamps frill the shorelines. It is a wild and secret place, and a hideout for all kinds of creatures, hunters and hunted.

A large cargo ship had pulled out of the Sasson dock, just south of the Indian Gateway, bound for Brunei. It was a long journey, and the crew was buzzing with excitement at rumours of her valuable cargo.

Had any of the crew ventured below and seen what they carried? Had they heard before of the Jewel of Bengal? Some had, and they were amazed and awestruck. But they would be at sea for many days. Would the priceless cargo be safe all that time?

News travels far and fast in the pirate world. There is always somebody somewhere, looking for an opportunity, gossiping with vulnerable sailors. And where there are prizes there are takers.

A small boat had hung in wait for some time, hidden amongst the dense vegetation of the mangrove swamps. The crew waited and waited, hovering patiently like vultures.

It was a warm dusk after a long, hot, sun-blistered day when the container showed itself as a tiny spot in the distance. Even from some miles away, it was vast. Heavy with cargo, it cut its route slowly through the water. The men gripped their weapons. This was it, they were sure. And when darkness fell, the sea vultures moved out into open water.

They would have to steer unseen across the open sea towards the

cargo ship, then scramble aboard noiselessly, climbing the bulk of the huge iron frame and avoiding the portholes as they went.

The first grapple hook launched upward and missed, hurtling back down, and splashing into the water. A moment to see if the alarm was raised, and then a second

attempt saw the hook curl itself neatly around the lower
railings. Then noiselessly the first man was on his way,
an empty bag on his back. One hand over the
other.

In a couple of breaths, his feet were
touching the deck. He'd made it.
Swiftly, he disappeared into the
shadowy interior of the ship.
The second man began his
ascent.

A low hatch was open
and knowing that his prize,
The Jewel of Bengal, would
be stored in the hold, the first
man knew he had to go deeper.
Avoiding lit staircases, he headed downwards,
slipping quietly from one darkened corner to another, until he reached the
inner bowels of the ship. The hold must be close now and with it, the prize
they had been so patiently waiting for.

The first man felt for a switch on the wall. There was nothing. But a
ring of keys hung on a hook and he took them gently. His hands fumbled
in the pitch black as he stretched out in front of him. Behind him, he heard
the sound of his friend's bare feet on the metal floor and he whispered
urgently, 'Find the light switch!'

Suddenly, he felt a sturdy lock in front of him. This must be it. He thought he heard a heaving sigh or an expelling of heavy breath, but he told himself that it must be imagination. Or maybe, his friend close behind him. Then a smell of musty, damp earth caught in his throat. The hold of a ship is not always the sweetest-smelling place to be.

His nerves taut, he jabbed the keys in the lock impatiently. He could not wait all night for his companion to find the light switch. Click. Eventually, he found the right key. The lock released and suddenly the door swung open. He walked forward uncertainly.

The floor beneath him seemed to move and change. It was soft, and yielding. Warm, even. Just then his friend muttered, 'I've found it.' And a light flickered on above them, illuminating the basement of the ship.

And at that moment, they realised that the Jewel of Bengal was not what they had expected. In front of them stood a beautiful white tiger. It rose to its feet, staring at the two men, its pale eyes blinking in the light. Then it licked its lips.

And so here
ends your journey my friend.
I hope my tales will dissuade you
from life at sea and you'll endeavour
to keep your heels dry.

But I'm goin' to be sailing these whale roads for a little

while longer. So, if you don't mind, I'll let you slip back

onto dry land and I'll carry along my way.

Wonderful tales by Chris Mould:

SHORTLISTED FOR THE CILIP KATE GREENAWAY MEDAL 2013

978 0 340 99935 6

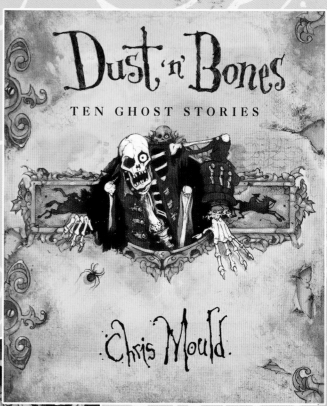

978 1 444 90617 2

978 1 444 90616 5